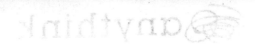

SPORTS **TO THE EXTREME**™

KITEBOARDING
AND SNOWKITING

Jeanne Nagle

rosen publishing's
**rosen
central**®

NEW YORK

Published in 2016 by The Rosen Publishing Group, Inc.
29 East 21st Street, New York, NY 10010

Library of Congress Cataloging in Publication Data

Nagle, Jeanne.
Kiteboarding and snowkiting/Jeanne Nagle.—First Edition.
    pages cm.—(Sports to the Extreme)
Includes bibliographical references and index.
ISBN 978-1-4994-3561-0 (Library bound)—ISBN 978-1-4994-3563-4 (Paperback)—
ISBN 978-1-4994-3564-1 (6-pack)
1. Kite surfing—Juvenile literature. I. Title.
GV840.K49N35 2015
797.3—dc23

2014047235

Manufactured in the United States of America

CONTENTS

INTRODUCTION

As the wind kicks up, the excitement builds. It's a breezy day at the beach, and the ocean curls and breaks in tempting, white-crested waves. Set apart from the crowds of sunbathers and swimmers is a group of people who are all thinking the same thing: it's a great day to fly a kite or surf the waves—or better yet, both at the same time. The conditions are just right to go kitesurfing, or kiteboarding.

Kites have been around for centuries. At various times, they have harnessed the wind to move vehicles, such as ships and carts, and even people. The sport of kite fighting has been around a while, as well. But the extreme sport of kitesurfing is pretty new. So is the cold-weather version of kitesurfing, known as kiteskiing, or kiteboarding.

Despite being fresh on the athletic scene, kitesurfing and kiteskiing—more accurately and popularly known as kiteboarding and snowkiting, respectively—have quickly become popular, especially with those people who are into board sports. That group includes surfers, windsurfers, and snowboarders, as well as water- and snow-skiers. They aren't the sports' only fans, though. People who enjoy other extreme sports would be good candidates to take part in kiteboarding and snowkiting events, too. In fact, anyone

Kiteboarders take to the air and surf on a beautiful day in Melbourne, Australia.

who thrills at the challenge of working with Mother Nature to ride the wind would enjoy these sports.

Along with that thrill, however, there is an element of danger. Kiteboarding and snowkiting are, after all, extreme sports. Beginners must receive plenty of training before attempting to ride a kite, and all participants—no matter their experience—need to take safety measures. These steps include using the right type of equipment, checking weather conditions, and performing with a clear head and attention to one's surroundings. When approached and handled correctly, kiteboarding and snowkiting are activities that can be enjoyed to the extreme.

CHAPTER ONE

BLOWING IN THE WIND

The start of what has become modern kiteboarding and snowkiting is interesting, although not 100 percent certain. There are stories about how people in ancient China—where kites were supposedly first invented—as well as in other parts of Asia, used kite-driven wind power to make their canoes and boats sail faster. One written tale from the Sui dynasty claims that Chinese emperor Wenxuan strapped winglike kites to prisoners' arms and made them jump off a tall tower. If any prisoner was lucky enough to float to the ground or over the city's wall, he would be freed. Apparently, no one ever did.

LIFT AND TRACTION

Some parts of the history of power kiting, which is what movement using kites and the wind has been called, are more certain. The world came closer to kiteboarding and snowkiting due to the experiments of a man named George Pocock.

Pocock was a teacher and inventor who lived in England during the late eighteenth and early nineteenth century. Fascinated by kites, he set out to prove that flying them could be more than a fun hobby. His idea was to have people move using wind power, where a kite or kites would pull people along in a vehicle of some kind. Pulling something in that way is called traction.

In 1824, Pocock attached a large kite that he had designed and built to a chair, then had his daughter sit in the chair. Wind power helped the kite move the seated girl several hundred feet into the air. Next, he attached kites to a carriage, creating a vehicle he called the charvolant. Rather than lift the carriage into the air, the kites were designed to pull it forward across the land.

This color engraving shows several charvolants (kite-drawn carriages) traveling along dirt roads under the power of the wind.

To do this, Pocock needed to control the action of the kites. He created a system using four strong lines that let him speed up, slow down, and steer. The four-line system that Pocock invented is very much like the controls used by modern-day kiteboarders and snowkiters.

"MAN-LIFTERS" GO TO WAR

Samuel Franklin Cody, an American living in England, began tinkering with kites at the turn of the twentieth century. Rather than using kites to pull someone in a vehicle, Cody's goal was to build a winged device that could lift a person to great heights, like a weather balloon. He wanted the British army to use his "man-lifter" kites to fly soldiers up over battlefields to observe the action during wartime. Cody's invention is important to kiteboarding and snowkiting because it helped prove that people could safely launch themselves up and land using a large kite.

Here you can see aviation pioneer Samuel Franklin Cody performing a test flight of his "Cody 1" powered airplane. Cody's previous aviation contributions included a man-lifter kite.

THE FATHERS OF KITEBOARDING

A number of developments took place from 1900 through the 1970s that would eventually affect kiteboarding and snowkiting. Most of them had to do with new materials for making kites and kite control lines. But the next big thing in the history of power kiting was centered in France in the 1980s, where a pair of brothers made a lasting mark on these types of sports.

Dominique and Bruno Legaignoux were French junior sailing champions who also liked to surf and wind-surf. While researching how to design a sail that would make their boats go faster, the brothers happened to see a catamaran being pulled speedily across the water by a large kite. From then on, the Legaignouxes had a passion for kite-powered sailing.

In 1984, the brothers designed their first kite built for water use. The kite was different from other water traction kites because it had bladders, or pockets, that were filled with air. These appendages allowed the Legaignouxes' kite to keep its crescent shape and not become waterlogged, which would keep it from

Bruno Legaignoux prepares for a kiteboard ride by filling an inflatable kite, which he and his brother Dominique invented.

taking off again once it had landed in the water. The air-filled bladders also helped the kite keep its shape when not in flight.

HANGING TEN (YEARS)

A year later, the brothers demonstrated their kite while riding the waves on water skis at Brest Speed Week, which is one stop on an international windsurfing tour. At the time, 1985, windsurfing was very popular. However, no one seemed particularly interested in kiteboarding. But the Legaignoux brothers believed in their invention and the new sport it would help create. For ten years, they worked on the kite, making it even better, continually trying to convince manufacturers and athletes to become interested in their product.

GIJSBERTUS ADRIANUS PANHUISE

The Legaignoux brothers may be the fathers of modern kiteboarding, but Dutchman Gijsbertus Adrianus Panhuise totally owned the sport. Or at least he kind of did, for a while. In 1977, Panhuise took out a patent on a wind-powered water sport that was similar to what became known as kiteboarding. His patent covered such details as a floating board and a parachute-like personal sail connected to the rider by a line attached to a harness, or belt. Nothing ever came of the patent, but Panhuise obviously influenced the creation of kiteboarding.

Then, in 1995, interest in windsurfing decreased and kiteboarding took off as a water sport. A Hong Kong company agreed to produce a limited number of inflatable kites, which sold well under the brand name Wipika. Luckily the brothers had patented their design, since the inflatable kite became the favorite for those enthusiasts taking part in the rising sport—and is still a preferred type today.

MEANWHILE, IN THE UNITED STATES . . .

At about the same time that the Legaignoux brothers were working on their first version of a surfing kite, American Corey Roeseler began developing a full kiteboarding system. Working with his father—a scientist with the aircraft company Boeing—Roeseler set about creating pieces of equipment that would work together to boost his kitesurfing speed.

At first Roeseler's kiteboarding system, which he called the KiteSki, consisted of a pair of water skis and a kite that was controlled using two lines attached to a steering bar. The bar was outfitted with a winch, which reeled in and let out the lines. A single board replaced the water skis early in the 1990s. Roeseler himself demonstrated the KiteSki in Hawaii in 1993, and the system became available for sale to the public in 1994.

WIND, SNOW, AND PARACHUTES IN GERMANY

What the Legaignoux brothers had done for kiteboarding, a German chemist and inventor named Dieter Strasilla did for the sport of snowkiting. He developed

a type of kite that pulled him up and down mountain slopes while on skis and also helped him glide across snow and ice in a controlled fashion.

Strasilla started experimenting with traction kiting in 1960, while he was in the United States. Using a parachute and an old pair of snow skis, he rode the desert dunes of White Sands

This lone figure glides over a snowy Bavarian hillside, courtesy of the wind and a fully inflated snowkite.

National Monument in New Mexico, being pulled along by wind power. By the early 1970s, he had developed a parachute-like kite that lifted him up and down the peaks of glaciers in the Swiss Alps.

Strasilla steered his kite—commonly called a paraglider—using long tethers (lines) running from the parachute to the rider beneath. Known also as the father of paragliding, which is flying using parachutes and the wind, Strasilla also did a fair bit of what could be considered kiteboarding in the '70s. Instead of being connected to a kite simply by lines and tethers, however, he soared over European lakes holding on to and steering using a solid metal bar. This type of paraglider was called a Skywing.

CATCHING AIR AND CATCHING ON

The sports of kiteboarding and snowkiting became increasingly popular as each new product was developed and demonstrated. Interest in kiteboarding was particularly high in Hawaii, where surfers and windsurfers found the new sport exciting and challenging. In 1998, a windsurfer, sail designer, and stunt-kite flyer named Joe Keuhl organized what is believed to be the first kiteboarding competition, off the island of Maui. Some twenty-five contestants competed in the event, which a man named Marcus "Flash" Austin won.

Professional surfer Laird Hamilton also helped make kiteboarding popular by becoming a fan of the sport and a kiteboarder himself. As one of the most high-profile surfers to start using kiteboards and testing their limits early on in the sport's history, Hamilton is considered a kiteboarding pioneer. In an article written in 2002 for *Windtracks* magazine, Hamilton spoke about his hopes for the future of kiteboarding. "I want to help establish the speed records for kitesurfing and sail around the world in a kiteboat," he told the writer. "There are no limits to what we can accomplish in this sport."

CHAPTER TWO

UP, UP, AND AWAY

Being good at kiteboarding or snowkiting requires skill and creativity. Mastering certain basic skills—such as how to launch, steer, stay in the air, touch down on the water/snow, and land safely—is the first step. From there, creativity comes into play as kiters attempt more complicated moves and tricks, including maneuvers they might invent themselves. Training is a huge part of gaining kiteboarding and snowkiting skills. Both skills and creativity are the result of practice.

WINDOW OF OPPORTUNITY

What makes power kiting sports extreme is lift and pull from the kite. Therefore, getting and keeping the kite airborne is a necessary and important first step when kiteboarding and snowkiting. Power kiters use their knowledge of the wind window to launch and fly safely.

A power kiter maneuvers his kite high overhead within the wind window. Knowing how to use the wind window is crucial to kiteboarding and snowkiting success.

The wind window is the section of the air in which the kite flies, courtesy of wind power. Shaped like a three-dimensional dome, the window extends downwind (in the same direction the wind is blowing) in front of and above the kiter. It is broken up into zones that determine how much lift and pull a kiter can get: the edge, the soft zone, and the power zone.

The edge of the window, which is the farthest away from the direct path of the wind that a kite can go while still staying inflated and aloft, is the zone with weak power but the most control and stability. This position lets the kite fill with air and rise but not violently pull the kiter forward or yank him or her straight up into the air. Launching as well as landing take place at the edge of the wind window.

Kiteboarders and snowkiters spend the most time flying in the middle area of the window, known as the soft zone. This position is a little more in the direct stream of the wind but still at an angle, so the kite is not being inflated full force.

When a kite is positioned in the middle of the window, directly in front of the kiter and receiving the full force of the wind, it is in the power zone. While it might seem as though the power zone would be the place to get the most out of kiteboarding and snowkiting, it is actually the zone that regular kiters use the least. The full force of the wind in a kite can be difficult to handle, even for experienced kiters. The power zone, then, is used mainly to relaunch when a kite has lost power and fallen into the water. Taking advantage of this area of the wind window is also how competitive kiters get the speed and height needed to perform spectacular stunts and tricks.

KITING WITH STYLE

Some people flock to kiteboarding and snowkiting to get a thrill from flying through the air and gliding across waves or snow drifts. But the

The sky above San Francisco Bay was brimming with kites as racers competed in the 2013 Kiteboard Racing North American Championships.

organized versions of these extreme sports revolve around races and other competitive events.

There are several styles of competitive power kiting. Both kiteboarding and snowkiting feature competitions centered on racing, where the emphasis is on speed, pure and simple. Pursuit races are when kiters go head-to-head against each other to see who can run a course and cross the finish line first. Course races, which are more common in kiteboarding competitions, set up markers that racers need to navigate while not losing speed. During a course race, large groups of kiteboarders are on the water at the same time and must be careful not to tangle their kite lines or crash into each other while traveling the course.

SPEED TRACKING

Snowkiters and kiteboarders are able to race against each other virtually thanks to Global Positioning System (GPS) technology. A personal tracking system records various power-kiting "runs," or sessions over a period of time. Kiters upload or otherwise submit their times to a supervising organization, which then ranks racers accordingly. GPS speed competitions are popular, but there are also events that track and rank distance.

TRICKY BUSINESS

Snowkiter Andy Wasinger practicing a trick in Alberta, Canada.

Course racing is all well and good, but freestyle, which is where kiters perform a variety of tricks, is where the real action is, on the water and in the snow. Each stunt has a specific degree of difficulty. Riders go through a series of routines, and judges rate their performance based on how well they did and how difficult their tricks were.

Competitive kiters add all sorts of special moves to their flying and gliding in order to impress judges during events, wow the crowd, and simply for their own enjoyment.

Most extreme kiteboarding and snowkiting tricks happen while the kiter is in the air. In order to get the serious hang time necessary to pull off these awesome moves, competitors put their jumping skills to the test.

JUMPS

Speed and timing are important to performing a jump. Once riders are moving at a good clip, they steer their kites smoothly upwind, meaning against the wind and in the opposite direction in which they are traveling. Just as the kite is almost directly over their heads, lifting them upward, they pull their boards, which are attached to their feet, out of the water or off the surface of the snow. In general, the greater the speed, the better the jump is bound to be.

GRABS, SPINS, AND LOOPS

Midjump is where many cool tricks are performed. Tricks that are recommended for beginners—after lots of practice, of course—include grabs, spins, and loops.

A grab is exactly what it sounds like. While in the air during a jump, the board rider reaches down and firmly grabs the board with one hand while maintaining control of the kite with the other. The grabbing arm should be as straight as possible, and the grab should be clearly held for as long as possible before landing. Grabs can be performed alone or in combination with other tricks, such as spins and loops.

Spins are when riders turn circles midair while standing on the board. Loop tricks involve the rider being up in the air while the kite does a quick loop-the-loop. To perform a good-looking spin or loop, riders want to move their weight back against one edge of the board so that it is up a bit out of the water going against the forward motion

RIDING THE RAILS

Borrowing moves from skateboarding and snowboarding, power kiters have been performing rail tricks for years. Rails are moves that feature a snowkiter sliding across a railing or a similar raised object. Rails, also called sliders, are frequently used maneuvers in snowkiting events. Freestyle kiteboarders have been known to use rails in their routines as well, but this kind of trick is more common during snowkiting.

of the kite. From there, riders take off into the air in what is known as a pop. The kite, which should be pretty close to overhead at this point, provides lift. Yet the pop happens mainly because of the rider's position on the board and his or her plain old determination to rise up out of the water or off the snow. Without the pop, the trick will fail.

WAVE RIDING AND SLALOM

Two other styles of power kiting are featured at kiteboarding competitions. Wave riding is basically the same as surfing, only with the extra punch added by using a kite for speed and lift. Contestants are judged on their speed and how smooth and fluid their rides are. Some of the bigger championship kiteboarding events—including those run by the Professional Kiteboard Riders Association (PKRA)—started adding slalom races in 2013. The slalom involves trying to outrace other competitors while maneuvering around set markers (buoys) along a water course.

CHAPTER THREE

GRAB SOME GEAR

It could be argued that even the most experienced, talented power kiters would be nothing without quality gear. Kites and boards have undergone radical changes over the years, with an eye toward giving riders an edge when it comes to speed, height, and the ability to maneuver as effortlessly as possible. Recognizing that kiteboarding and snowkiting are loaded with risk, there also has been a push to emphasize and upgrade related safety gear as well.

HOW THINGS HAVE SHAPED UP

One of the key pieces of equipment necessary to take part in these extreme sports is, of course, a kite. Traction kites have come a long way since George Pocock strapped a couple of saillike devices onto a carriage back in the 1800s. They have even advanced in the relatively few years since Bruno and Dominique Legaignoux designed the first successful inflatable kite. In fact, the Legaignoux brothers continued to design kites for years and even managed to top themselves.

The first kite that the brothers designed had a rigid leading edge (the part that goes into the wind first) caused by the inflatable bladders. The stiff leading edge, combined with lines attached to each of the four corners, made the kite look like a flying letter C. The shape in flight is why this design is called a C kite. While C kites were better than other types of traction kites that had come before, there were still some problems. Chief among the trouble spots was the fact that although the bladders kept the kite afloat, C kites could still be hard to relaunch from the water.

Bruno Legaignoux designs kites at his office in the Dominican Republic. The Legaignoux brothers have continued to refine and improve their kites.

To combat the relaunch issue, the Legaignoux brothers designed what has become known as the bow kite. With a leading edge similar to the C kite, the bow kite was different because of its concave trailing edge, meaning its "back end" was curved inward slightly. Also, lines were not attached directly to a bow kite, but rather to a bridle, or frame on the leading edge that helped steady the kite for flying. Their trailing edge and bridle gave bow kites a much flatter flying shape than C kites, and, therefore, they were easier to manage during a water relaunch. Bow kites also are easier to "depower," which can keep a kiter from going too fast or being dragged and injured after wiping out or falling.

Not only do kites come in different styles, they also come in various sizes. As a general rule, the larger the kite, the more power. Smaller kites, however, are better when there is only a little wind because it takes less wind to get them moving. Most kites, no matter their shape or size, are sold with kite line and a bar for steering. A pump is generally also included in the price of inflatable kites.

INFLATE OR FOIL?

Foil kites have a soft-cell design that makes them look and operate more like parachutes than traditional kites.

As mentioned, inflatable kites are awesome for kiteboarding because they don't sink in the water. Inflatables may be used for snowkiting as well, but the floating issue isn't so important in the snow. Many snowkiters use a different kind of kite in the ice and snow, called a foil.

Despite the name, a foil kite is not actually made of foil but of polyester or similar fabrics. The name is short for "parafoil," which is kind of like a parachute. Instead of a rigid leading edge or a bridle, foils have soft cells that fill with wind to keep them up in the air. The cells give foil kites a ridged or paneled look. Snowkiters like using foils because they are lighter and easier to manage in some ways. Foils need very little wind power to work well and are even better at depowering than inflatable bow kites. Also, there's no need to carry a pump to inflate bladders before use.

EARNING SOME KITE CHOPS

Power-kite experts, meaning instructors and manu-facturers, recommend that beginning kiteboarders and snowkiters get a feel for flying while staying grounded. Training kites let extreme-sport hopefuls learn how to manage the pull and power of the wind window without risking their necks out in the open water or on the side of a mountain.

Training kites are basically simpler, scaled-down versions of power kites. They are smaller—usually no larger than thirty-two square feet (three square meters)—and there are only two lines, instead of four, to handle. Beginners can simply plant their feet in a park or field and practice their steering and con-trol. Once they get the hang of navigating the wind window, they can further test their skills by strapping on some skates or climbing on a skateboard for a dry run or two.

THE BOARD GAME

When it comes to choosing a board for kiteboarding, one size (or style) does not fit all. Boards are designed for different purposes and kinds of riding. There are boards meant to bring the best to wave riding, racing, and freestyle tricks.

Wave boards are perhaps the most like a traditional surfboard—which makes sense because, after all, surfing is basically wave riding. Like a surfboard, a wave board has fins, which is a part attached to the bottom of the board that helps with steering. Beginners should take advantage of optional straps and footholds on some wave boards so that they stand the best chance of staying upright and not losing track of the board if they fall off.

Riding style and personal preference should help kiteboarders figure out which type of board features—such as footholds—are right for them.

Racing boards are built for speed. Their shape is streamlined, meaning it is curved and smoothed so that it cuts through the water easily and quickly. That includes the rocker, which is a bowed shape running the length of the bottom of the board. Rockers help boards better turn and cut through—or "carve," in surf speak—the water by matching the shape of the board with natural curls of waves.

Freestyle kiteboarders usually prefer to use twin-tip boards. The "twin" in their name comes from having two ends that are exactly the same. Other types of boards have a specific nose and tail and are designed to be ridden nose first. Because there is no nose or tail, twin-tip boards can be ridden in either direction without the rider having to doing switch positions. This makes doing tricks easier, as well as maintaining general balance and control.

Snowkiters are able to use just about any regular snowboard, but there are some things they should consider before choosing a board. Riders need to buy a board that is a good fit for their size and weight. Also, they should consider what the snow and wind conditions will be where they plan to snowkite. Will there be fluffy, powdery snow or packed ice? Will the area be mainly flat, gently sloped, or with high cliffs to fly up and down? Does the rider plan on doing lots of tricks or concentrating mainly on speed? All these things can influence what size and make of board one chooses. Some snowkiters go the traditional route and use skis instead of snowboards.

SAFETY FIRST, LAST, AND ALWAYS

Kiteboarding and snowkiting are thrilling sports, but they are also dangerous, no matter who is flying the kite. Beginners and professionals alike need to take certain steps to ensure they do not get injured or die while competing or having some fun. One of those steps is to make sure they bring along proper safety gear when they ride the wind.

KITING INSURANCE

Beyond using proper safety gear, and making sure "the coast is clear" when launching and landing, power kiters can protect themselves and others by purchasing some insurance. There are policies that cover extreme sports and others that are power kite specific. Kiteboarders and snowkiters might also wish to contact their insurance carriers to see if they can add coverage to the carrier's existing policies. Some organizations, such as the British Powerkiting Association and the United States Kitesurfing Association, offer free or price-reduced policies as part of their membership dues.

Some of the gear used to protect kiteboarders and snowkiters is the same that can be found on athletes in other extreme sports—and even some nonextreme ones. These include helmets, knee pads, and elbow pads. Additional "crash-guard" clothing, such as impact vests and shorts, are also a good idea, especially for beginners.

Other safety equipment is geared more closely to the needs of kite and board riders specifically. For instance, many riders wear harnesses that are attached to the kite in order to give extra support to the arms, which are controlling the kite as it is pushed and pulled by the wind. These harnesses are equipped with a safety release that lets a rider quickly disconnect from and depower the kite in dangerous conditions.

This kiteboarder enjoys a safe ride while wearing a harness. Many kiteboarding professionals recommend that beginners, in particular, take advantage of such safety measures.

Sometimes the environment in which the sport takes place can be threatening as well. Like skiing and snowboarding, snowkiting can take people into remote areas where ice and snow could become harmful. Carrying a radio to call for help and snowshoes in case the rider needs to walk instead of glide back to safety are two reasonable options for snowkiters. An avalanche kit, with things such as beacons and a small shovel, is not out of the question either.

CHAPTER FOUR

TOUR AND LEARN

Kiteboarders and snowkiters face a variety of opponents, depending on their level of experience (and expertise). Professional board-sport athletes, and even amateurs who enter competitions, obviously try to outperform others in their sport during any given event. Those who take to the water or slopes mainly for fun and thrills go up against Mother Nature. After all, dealing with unpredictable weather and potentially dangerous natural conditions is part of what makes these extreme sports.

However, all powerkiters have a challenger in common—themselves. Those who are active in kiteboarding and snowkiting are constantly looking to increase their speed and improve their overall performance, whether

These power kiters take advantage of winds whipped up by an approaching storm, complete with a bank of dark, threatening clouds.

they are pros kiting at an organized event or beginners trying to push new boundaries.

Professional associations can help kiteboarders and snowkiters of every experience level achieve their athletic goals. These organizations sponsor events; offer training (and certification for trainers); and provide lots of information about the latest equipment, tricks, and personalities, and general news about the sports.

GAINING TRACTION

When kiteboarding, and later snowkiting, started as an organized sport, events were staged by individuals on pretty much an occasional basis. Some of the first organizers, such as Joe Keuhl, put in not only their time but also their own money to get an event off the ground. Keuhl recalls that he put up $400 of his own money when pulling together his first race, which is considered to be the very first kiteboarding event in the history of the sport. But he believed it was money well spent because it really kicked the sport into high gear.

"We pulled off a cool event that got great coverage from the photographers and writers of the surf rags," Keuhl told *The Kiteboarder* magazine in 2007. "The big sponsors came the following year with their lawyers and took it even further."

Today, thanks to sponsors such as Red Bull and board manufacturer Cabrinha, competitive kiteboarding and snowkiting are going strong and even picking up speed. Events are popping up in locations as far-flung as China, Africa, Switzerland, and Russia, as well as across Europe and North America. In fact, kiteboarding and snowkiting are practiced as organized extreme sports, with official events, on six of the world's seven continents. The only holdout as of the end of 2014 is Antarctica. But snowkiters have been known to ride the frozen tundra there for the thrill of it, so can an organized competition in Antarctica be too far behind?

FRÉDÉRIC DION

In February 2014, Canadian adventurer Frédéric Dion earned the world record for kiteskiing continuously in a twenty-four-hour period. By traveling nearly 373 miles (600 km), Dion beat the previous record for this event, set in 2010, by about 3 miles (5 km). Continuing his snowkiting adventures, Dion set out in November 2014 to kiteski alone to the center of Antarctica, across territory called the Pole of Inaccesibility. Other adventurers have snowkited this route, but in groups, not solo.

As the image of this lone kiter in Wisconsin attests, snowkiting can be a solitary experience. The isolation is no problem for Frédéric Dion, though, who has met several solo snowkiting challenges.

KITEBOARDING ON TOUR

The International Kiteboarding Association (IKA) is an organization that makes rules regarding kiteboarding competitions around the world. Under the supervision of the International Sailing Federation, the IKA has the power to make or break high-ranking kiteboarding tours. These are the competitions that award national and world championship titles.

There are only a few kiteboarding tours that are sanctioned, or officially approved of and supported, by the IKA. These cover tour events put on by the Professional Kite Riders Association (PKRA), the Kitesurf Tour Europe (KTE), Kiteboard Tour Asia (KTA), and Kite Surf Pro (KSP).

PKRA

The PKRA is responsible for nearly eighty events that draw kiteboarders to exotic locations around the globe every year. Among these are the competitions of the World Kiteboarding Tour. Stops on the tour include several "world cup" events and the popular Fuerteventura grand slam in the Canary Islands. The PKRA has given millions in prize money to winners of their events.

KTE

Formed in 2010, the KTE states that its purpose is "to bring kitesurfing to the people." Kiteboarders compete in teams made up of three riders, one of whom is female. Judging at KTE events concentrates heavily on creative tricks and air time. Partly because the group is still pretty new, there are not as many events on the KTE schedule as there are on the more established PKRA tour. Past sponsors of tour events include MINI, the British car brand (as in the Mini Cooper), and candy maker Chupa Chups.

KTA

Asia is the focus of the KTA. Like the European tour, the KTA is a relative newcomer, formed in 2009. Competitions are set up in as many Asian countries as possible each year. Event sites in 2014 included Taiwan, the Philippines, and Tajikistan. The KTA hosted the 2013 IKA World Championships in China, the first time the event had taken place in Asia. In addition to competitive events, the organization also sponsors training and clinics, including the safety-focused Kite Kids program.

Kiteboarders face off against each other and the elements during a 2014 KTA event off Trikora Beach on Bintan Island, Indonesia.

KSP

Created by four kiteboarding world champs, the KSP tour focuses on wave riding events. A handful of competitions at such varied locales as Portugal, Ireland, and the island nation of Mauritius lead kiteboarders to the title event, the Kite Surf Pro World Championship, in Maui.

THE COLLEGIATE KITEBOARDING ASSOCIATION

In 2003, a group of college-age kiteboarders on spring break in the Florida Keys pulled together a competitive event on the spur of the moment. That first event led to more planned, organized competitions that spread along the East Coast and across the country to the West Coast as well. Thus the Collegiate Kiteboarding Association (CKA) was born.

The CKA still stages a yearly event in the Keys, as well as other locations in Florida, Georgia, South Carolina, Oregon, and California. All these lead to the CKA National Championships, held in June, after the collegiate school year has ended. In 2014, the CKA started a scholarship fund to help riders afford participation in CKA events. A high school riders division and a snowkiting event were added for the 2014–2015 season.

TOPS IN THE SNOW

Snowkiters can choose to participate in any number of regional, national, and international events, which are held mainly in the winter months. Racers at the International Snowkite Championships, usually held in Reschensee, Italy, compete for freestyle and race titles. In the United States and Canada, a series of events held in both countries are grouped together into the North American Snowkite Tour. Snowkiters participate in as many races as possible to earn points in both freestyle and racing divisions. After the last event has been held, the points are added up and the person with the most points wins the championship title.

GETTING SCHOOLED

Participants in kiteboarding and snowkiting tours and events are either professionals or amateurs who have a lot of experience. Of course, people can ride power kites on their own, without taking part in an organized event. But not competing is no excuse not to train to get better. Training and lessons are necessities, especially for anyone who has never taken part in an extreme power-kiting sport.

Anyone who has experience surfing, wakeboarding, or even sailing should have an easier time kiteboarding than an absolute beginner. Likewise, snowboarders and skiers are at somewhat of an advantage when they decide to try snowkiting. However—and this cannot be stressed enough—kiteboarding and snowkiting are totally different sports from any of those other activities. The play of the kite in the wind window makes riding a board or skis a whole new experience.

The best way to learn is to take lessons from someone who has logged a lot of hours flying a power kite. Some sources estimate that each lesson can cost as much as $100. Multiply that by at least ten one-hour sessions and it's easy to see that kiteboarding and snowkiting lessons are not exactly cheap. Still, training is well worth the money if riders gain experience and stay safe.

People just about anywhere can take power-kite lessons. As noted in a 2010 article in *Newsweek*, "Kitesurfing schools can be found in such far-flung places as Kenya, Vietnam, Patagonia, and even a lagoon outside Dakhla, Morocco, in the middle of the Sahara."

A FINAL WORD

The popularity of kiteboarding seemed to reach a peak in 2012, when it was announced that the sport would replace wind-surfing at the 2016 Olympic Games in Rio de Janeiro, Brazil. Almost as quickly as that news was announced, however, the Olympic Committee retook the vote, and kiteboarding was out, windsurfing back on the schedule.

Kiteboarders and their fans have vowed to get their sport back on the Olympic events list by 2020. Still others would like to see kite-boarding and snowkiting at the X Games—where many people think they belonged in the first place, not at the Olympics.

Wherever these extreme sports may land in the future, they are bound to keep flying high and strong in the hearts of their supporters, participants, and fans, both those in the present and many others yet to come.

GLOSSARY

bladder A bag or tube that can be filled with air or water.

bridle In kiting, a frame to which a kite line is attached.

catamaran A type of sailing vehicle that has a deck connected to two, separate floating bodies.

collegiate Something that has to do with college or those who go to college.

downwind In the same direction that the wind is blowing.

freestyle A competition in which participants use different styles of their own choosing.

harness A belt and strap that connect a person to an object, such as a power kite.

launch To send something into the air.

leading edge The part of a power kite that goes into the wind first.

paraglider A type of parachute that is changed so that someone can use it like a kite to fly gently through the air.

sanction To officially approve of and support something.

sponsor To give money or other types of support so that an event can take place.

stability The state of being strong, balanced, and in good condition.

tether A line of some kind that is meant to keep an object from moving too far away from a certain location.

traction Describes the power to move an object.

trailing edge The part of a kite that goes into the wind last, or the "back end."

upwind Toward the direction from which the wind is blowing.

FOR MORE INFORMATION

Canadian Kiteboarding Association (CKA)
Collingwood, ON
Canada
E-mail: canadakite@gmail.com
Website: https://www.facebook.com/CanadaKite
Formed in 2011, the CKA supervises kiteboarding activities
throughout Canada. A member organization of the Interna-
tional Kiteboarding Federation, the CKA helps organize events,
enforces rules, and maintains Canadian national rankings in
the sport.

Canadian Kite Surfing Society
Toronto, ON
Canada
(416) 898-3859
Website: http://ckss.ca
The Canadian Kite Surfing Society (CKSS) has written into its
mission that it wants to "share our knowledge of the sport."
CKSS programs that do just that include equipment sales and
repair, newsletters, and lessons at every level of ability.

International Kiteboarding Association
Rohrbecker Weg 43
Falkensee
14612
Germany
Website: http://internationalkiteboarding.org
The IKA sets and regulates the rules for all officially sanctioned
kiteboarding events. The organization also schedules events,
posts results and rankings, and communicates important
information regarding competitions and official policies.

International Sailing Federation
Ariadne House
Town Quay
Southampton
Hampshire
SO14 2AQ
United Kingdom
Website: http://www.sailing.org
The International Sailing Federation, which is the governing body for the sport of sailing worldwide, oversees the work of the International Kiteboarding Association. Among its duties, the federation offers advice and guidance to a windsurfing and kiteboarding committee, which helps develop and promote board-sailing sports.

United States Extreme Sports Association
6350 Lake Oconee Parkway
Suite 102-128
Greensboro, GA 30642
(877) 900-8737 (toll free)
Website: http://usesa.org
The United States Extreme Sports Association is an umbrella organization for extreme sports communities. It overseas discounts on equipment and services and hosts an extreme-sports social network.

United States Kiteboarder Association
Kennewick, WA

(509) 734-8014

Website: http://www.USKiteboarderAssociation.com

The United States Kiteboarder Association is a member organization designed to create and maintain enthusiasm for the sport. USKA leadership maintains partnerships with equipment manufacturers, kiteboarding schools, and certified instructors to the benefit and safety of all North American riders.

WEBSITES

Because of the changing nature of Internet links, Rosen Publishing has developed an online list of websites related to the subject of this book. This site is updated regularly. Please use this link to access the list:

http://www.rosenlinks.com/STTE/Kite

FOR FURTHER READING

David, Jack. *Kiteboarding.* Minneapolis, MN: Bellwether Media, 2009.

Herzog, Brad. *E Is for Extreme: An Extreme Sports Alphabet.* Chelsea, MI: Sleeping Bear Press, 2007.

Laval, Anne-Marie. *Windsurfing and Kite Surfing.* Mankato, MN: Smart Apple Media, 2012.

Mattern, Joanne. *Kiteboarding* (Action Sports). Vero Beach, FL: Rourke Publishing Group, 2008.

Thomas, Carter, et al. *The Kiteboarder Magazine Beginner Instructional Guide.* Los Osos, CA: The Kiteboarder Magazine, 2013.

Thomas, Isabelle. *Board Sports: The Boarders, the Tricks, the Lingo.* Minneapolis, MN: Lerner Publications Company, 2011.

BIBLIOGRAPHY

ArticlesBase. "Corey Roeseler—The Greatest Kiteboarding Legend." June 2012. Retrieved October 2014 (http://www.articlesbase .com/water-sports-articles/cory-roeseler-the-greatest-kiteboarding -legend-6003127.html).

Backer, Stina. "Kiteboarding: Meet Future Champions of Newest Olympic Sport." CNN online, July 2012. Retrieved October 2014 (http://edition.cnn.com/2012/07/06/sport/kiteboarding -olympics-champions/index.html).

Bowe, Tucker. "Primer: The Winds and Waves of Kiteboarding." *Gear Patrol*, September 2014. Retrieved October 2014 (http:// gearpatrol.com/2014/09/04/primer-beginners-guide-to -kiteboarding).

Boyce, Jeremy. *The Ultimate Book of Power Kiting and Kiteboarding.* Guilford, CT: The Lyons Press, 2004.

Campbell, Peter. "Kitesurfing Handbook." Peter's Kitesurfing Blog. Retrieved October 2014 (http://kitesurfing-handbook .peterskiteboarding.com/a/peterskiteboarding.com/kitesurfing -handbook).

Coetzer, Correne. "ExWeb Interview with Frederic Dion, Invention and Modification for the South Pole of Inaccesibility." Polar Explorersweb, November 2014. Retrieved November 2014 (http://www.explorersweb.com/polar/news.php?url=exweb- interview-with-frederic-dion_1414965617).

Collegiate Kiteboarding Association. "About Us. " Retrieved November 2014 (http://collegekiteboarding.com/about-us).

Epikoo. "Chupa Chups Sponsors Kitesurf Tour Europe (KTE)." April 2012. Retrieved November 2014 (http://epikoo.com/ kiteboarding/news/chupa-chups-sponsors-kitesurf-tour-europe -kte).

Govig, Valerie. "Harness the Wind: Kite Power." *Omni*, March 1994.

GPS Kitesurfing. "Information and Rules." Retrieved November 2014 (http://www.gps-kitesurfing.com/default.aspx?mnu=item&item=website).

Guo, Jerry. "The Next Extreme Sport." *Newsweek International*, September 6, 2010.

The Kiteboarder School. "Basic Kiteboarding Skills." Retrieved November 2014 (http://thekiteboarderschool.com/basic-kiteboarding-jumps).

Kiteboarder Zone. 2012 Kite Surf Pro Tour Schedule. February 2012. Retrieved November 2014 (http://www.kiteboarderzone.com/magazines/sbc-kiteboard-magazine/2159-2012-ksp-tour-schedule.html).

Kiteboarding Evolution. "The Kiteboarding Kite." Retrieved November 2014 (http://www.kiteboardingevolution.com/kiteboarding-kite.html).

Kiteboarding Evolution. "What Are Trainer Kites?" Retrieved October 2014 (http://www.kiteboardingevolution.com/trainer-kites.html).

Lang, Paul. "Who Is Joe Cool?" *The Kiteboarder*, September 2007. Retrieved November 2014 (http://www.thekiteboarder.com/2007/09/who-is-joe-cool-extended-feature).

Lapierre, Adam. "'Roots of Kiteboarding' Next in Sense of Place Series." *Hood River News*, October 2013. Retrieved October 2014 (http://www.hoodrivernews.com/news/2012/oct/09/roots-kiteboarding-next-sense-place-series).

Mathis, Brandon. "What Is a Directional Twin Snowboard?" Livestrong.com, March 2013. Retrieved November 2014 (http://www.livestrong.com/article/508719-what-is-a-directional-twin-snowboard).

McWilliams, Paul. "A Guide to Safety Gear for Snowkiting." Snowkiting Holidays.com, September 2014. Retrieved October 2014 (http://snowkitingholidays.com/gear/a-guide-to-safety-gear-for-snowkiting).

North American Snowkite Tour. "About." Retrieved November 2014 (http://www.snowkitetour.com/about).

Professional Kite Riders Association. "About the PKRA." Retrieved October 2014 (http://www.prokitetour.com/about-pkra.php).

Snowkite World Cup. "The Snowkite World Championship Is Set to Reschensee." January 2010. Retrieved November 2014 (http://www.surfertoday.com/kiteboarding/2884-the-snowkite-world -championship-is-set-to-reschensee).

Surf Science. "Different Rocker Shapes." Retrieved November 2014 (http://www.surfscience.com/topics/surfboard-anatomy/rocker/ different-rocker-shapes).

Thornton, T. D. "Snowkiting Is Beginning to Take Off." *Boston Globe*, February 2008. Retrieved October 2014 (http://www.boston.com/ travel/explorene/specials/ski/articles/2008/02/21/snowkiting_is _beginning_to_take_off).

Tronet, Jeremy. "Loop That Kite: How to Loop a Kite." *The Kiteboarder*, December 2009. Retrieved November 2014 (http://www. thekiteboarder.com/2009/12/loop-that-kite-how-to-kite-loop).

VanderZee, Jake. "Closed vs. Open Cell Kites for Kiteboarding and Snowkiting." MACKite. Retrieved November 2014 (http://www .mackiteboarding.com/closed-vs-open-cell-foil-kites-for-kiteboarding -and-snow-kiting.htm).

White, Diamond. "The Bow Kite." Inflatablekite.com, October 2005 Retrieved November 2014 (http://inflatablekite.com/sitebow/ BowHome.html).

White, Diamond. "The Kiteboarding History." Inflatablekite.com, May 2006. Retrieved October 2014 (http://inflatablekite.com/siteinf/ gb/InfHistory.html).

Yates, Brad. "The Kite Story on Maui." HiLevel Coaching: Athletes. August 2002. Retrieved October 2014 (http://bradyates.com/mt/ archives/2002/08/the_kite_story.html).

INDEX

ABOUT THE AUTHOR

After thoroughly researching this book, author Jeanne Nagle wishes she were better at ski and board sports, so as to experience power kiting herself. Among the other Rosen titles she has written are *Careers in Coaching*; *Archie, Peyton, and Eli Manning* (Sports Families); : *Sidney Crosby* (Living Legends of Sports); and *Extreme Biking* (Sports to the Extreme).

PHOTO CREDITS

Cover, p. 4 (kiteboarder) © iStockphoto.com/LifesizeImages; cover, pp. 1, 3, 7, 15, 22, 30 (wave) © iStockphoto.com/irabell; p. 5 Craig Sillitoe/Getty Images; p. 8 Science & Society Picture Library/Getty Images; p. 9 Daily Herald Archive/SSPL/Getty Images; pp. 10, 23 Bloomberg/Getty Images; pp. 12–13 Timm Schamberger/AFP/DDP/Getty Images; p. 16 Luis Davilla/Photodisc/Getty Images; p. 18 Ezra Shaw/Getty Images; p. 19 Kurtis Kristanson/Sports Studio Photos/Getty Images; p. 24 © iStockphoto.com/lily3; p. 26 Pam Francis/Photographer's Choice/Getty Images; p. 29 Cultura RM/Jakob Helbig/Getty Images; p. 30 (inset) Mike Theiss/National Geographic Image Collection/Getty Images; p. 32 Robert Stebler/Moment/Getty Images; p. 34 Yuli Seperi/Getty Images; cover and interior pages graphics SkillUp/Shutterstock.com, Sfio Cracho/Shutterstock.com, saide/Shutterstock.com, Frank Rohde/Shutterstock.com, Thomas Bethge/Shutterstock.com, nortivision/Shutterstock.com, PinkPueblo/Shutterstock.com.

Designer: Michael Moy; Executive Editor: Hope Lourie Killcoyne